Primary Ecology Series

How Trees Help Me

Bobbie Kalman & Janine Schaub

 Crabtree Publishing Company

The Primary Ecology Series

To Thomas Adams

Writing team
Bobbie Kalman
Janine Schaub

Editor-in-chief
Bobbie Kalman

Editor
Shelagh Wallace

Design and computer layout
Antoinette "Cookie" DeBiasi

Cover mechanicals
Diane Coderre

Type output
Lincoln Graphics

Photo processing
Ray J. Kunnapuu/Heritage Images

Color separations
ISCOA

Artwork and cover design:
Antoinette "Cookie" DeBiasi
Artwork: page 24 by Lynne Carson

Photographs:
Bobbie Kalman and Antoinette DeBiasi: Cover, title page, pages 5, 8 (top), 10, 11 (bottom), 14, 17 (bottom), 20, 21, 24, 25 (bottom), 28-31
Peter Crabtree: pages 7 (bottom), 9 (bottom), 11 (top), 17 (top), 19 (top)
Jim Bryant: page 4
Andre Baude: pages 7 (top), 9 (top), 22
Greg Robinson: pages 8 (bottom), 16, 25 (top)
Diane Majumdar: page 6
Carol Stewart: page 23
Crabtree Publishing Company made every effort to secure model releases.

"The troll and the tree" and the activity **"How to 'troll' a tree"** were written by Chris Taylor.

Printer
Lake Book Manufacturing

Special thanks to: Jackie Stafford, Beryl Tupman, Cindee Karnick-Davison, the students of Elmlea Junior School and Parliament Oak Elementary School, Melissa and Katie Drohan, Ashley Caldwell, Ian Hawksbee, Rebecca Prewitt, Justin Hope, Richard Wilkinson, (the following children are shown on the front cover) Erin Wiltshire, N'Kruma Hylton, Lavanniyah Satkunarajah, Jenny To, Elena Rusu, Sunil Dat Neelbarran, Shawn Harris. Pamela Combden appears on the back cover.

Published by
Crabtree Publishing Company

350 Fifth Avenue	6900 Kinsmen Court	73 Lime Walk
Suite 3308	P.O. Box 1000	Headington
New York	Niagara Falls, ON	Oxford OX3 7AD
N.Y. 10118	Canada L2E 7E7	United Kingdom

Cataloguing in Publication Data
Kalman, Bobbie, 1947-
   How trees help me

(The Primary ecology series)
Includes index.
ISBN 0-86505-554-8 (library bound) ISBN 0-86505-580-7 (pbk.)

1. Trees - Juvenile literature.
2. Trees - Environmental aspects - Juvenile literature.
3. Ecology - Juvenile literature.
I. Schaub, Janine. II. Title. III. Series.

QK475.8.K35 1992   j582.16

Contents

4   Trees are important to the earth

6   What is a tree?

8   Coniferous and broadleaved trees

10   From the roots up

12   Tree-leaf quiz

14   The story of the ginkgo tree

16   Flowers, fruits, and cones

18   A tree is born

20   How a tree dies

22   Dangers to trees

24   How you can help trees

26   The troll and the tree

28   How to "troll" a tree

30   Make friends with a tree

32   Glossary and Index

Trees are important to the earth

Trees are important wherever they grow. The food for many animals and insects comes from the bark, sap, leaves, seeds, fruit, and flowers of trees. Trees provide food even when they die. They break down and form a rich substance that adds nutrition to the earth. The nutrition from dead trees feeds growing plants.

Forests are very important to the environment. They can be found in mountain, wetland, and tropical areas of the world. Forests keep the air moist and fresh and provide homes for millions of creatures.

Controlling soil and water

The roots of trees hold soil in place. Without trees, soil would be washed away when it rained. Trees also help control water. They prevent floods and keep the areas around them from turning into deserts.

When it rains in a forest, only half of the rainwater reaches the ground. Some is absorbed by the bark of trees; some stays on the leaves and evaporates back into the air. The water that reaches the ground is held by the roots of the tree, keeping the soil around it moist.

Many animals make their homes and find food in trees. This monkey lives in the rainforest.

How trees help us

Trees are important to people in other ways, too. People like to live where there are trees because the air is fresh, and trees give them shelter from the sun and wind.

People all over the world depend on trees for food, wood, paper, and fuel. The pencil you are using and the book you are reading were made from trees. Look around you and count all the things that came from trees. The house in which you live, your school, and your furniture are largely made from wood. Half of the medicines in the world came from rainforests! Forests contain cures for diseases that do not yet have cures. Trees are our friends. Give one a hug today!

What is a tree?

Trees come in all shapes, sizes, and colors. Some are big enough to climb, and some are as tiny and frail as wildflowers. Some trees have leaves, and others have needles. Some have flowers or fruit; others have cones. Even though there are so many different kinds of trees, all trees are plants that grew from a single woody stem and have trunks, roots, branches, and leaves.

Banyan trees sprout pillar roots from their branches. The roots grow downward, take hold in the soil, and grow as separate trunks. The oldest banyan tree (shown below) is in India. It has grown so many trunks that it has become a forest all by itself!

Not all trees look the way we expect them to look. What shapes can you see in this forest?

Many fruits come from trees. Spices, syrup, and chocolate are also gifts from trees.

Gifts from trees

People have been planting trees for thousands of years. Trees give us many of the foods we eat each day, such as fruits and nuts. Spices and medicines also come from trees. Cinnamon, for example, is made from the inner bark of the laurel tree. The seeds from the cacao tree are dried, roasted, and ground up into paste, which is used in making chocolate. Tea, cof̲̲̲̲̲̲̲̲̲̲̲̲̲̲̲̲ber, chewing gum, olive oil, m̲̲̲̲̲̲̲rup, and paper are all products tha̲̲̲̲ from trees.

Coniferous and broadleaved trees

Although trees often look quite different, all trees belong to two groups: **coniferous** and **broadleaved** trees.

Coniferous trees

Coniferous trees are trees with cones and needles. Most are evergreens. They are called "evergreen" because they stay green all year. They do not shed all their leaves each season but replace them a few at a time. The needles of coniferous trees have a waxy coating that keeps water from evaporating.

Many tropical broadleaved trees are evergreens but, in cold areas, evergreens are usually coniferous, such as the trees below.

(above) Coniferous trees have cones and waxy needles. They do not shed their leaves in winter but replace them a few at a time.

In tropical areas of the world, broadleaved trees keep their leaves all year because there is plenty of water available for making food.

Broadleaved trees

Broadleaved trees have wide, flat leaves. These trees can be found all over the world. Some broadleaved trees are called **deciduous** trees. Deciduous trees are flowering trees that shed all their leaves during one season. Their thin leaves give off water that cannot be replaced in cold weather. They cannot make food during this time because there is not enough sunshine or water for making food.

The leaves of deciduous trees turn spectacular colors in autumn.

From the roots up

Roots keep trees from falling over. They anchor trees into the ground. Roots also collect the food and water that a tree needs to survive. Under the ground, the tree's roots sprout millions of tiny threads called **root hairs**. Root hairs absorb water and food from the soil. They grow to their full length in a month or two and then die. As they are growing and dying, the roots of the tree get longer and thicker. These thick roots take food from the root hairs up through the tree's trunk.

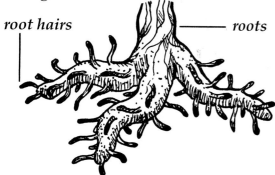

root hairs ———— roots

Through the trunk

The trunk of a tree is round and covered with bark. Water and nutrients are carried from the roots to the leaves in little tubes that are deep inside the trunk. The food that trees need is made in the leaves and is taken back down to the roots through other tubes that are found under the bark all around the tree.

Bark—a tree's skin

Bark is the tree's skin. Young trees have smooth bark; old trees have rough bark. Each tree has two layers. The bark that you can see and touch is the oldest part of the tree. It protects the tree trunk and branches. Just under the outer layer of bark is the second layer of growing bark. As new bark forms, the outer bark splits, making the trunk look cracked.

Green leaves, fresh air

The leaves of most trees are green. The special substance inside leaves that makes them green is called **chlorophyll**. In an almost magical way, chlorophyll makes food for trees.

A tree makes its food from air, sunlight, and water. Sunlight and chlorophyll change air and water into **sap**, the food that makes trees grow.

A breath of fresh air

When we breathe in, we use a gas called **oxygen** that is part of the air. When we breathe out, we get rid of a gas called **carbon dioxide**. Carbon dioxide is also produced by cars and factories. Too much carbon dioxide is harmful to people, animals, birds, fish, insects, and plants.

When trees breathe through their leaves, they use carbon dioxide. After trees have used carbon dioxide from the air, they give off large amounts of oxygen. Forests all over the world constantly supply the earth with clean air. Without trees, our air would not be good enough to breathe, and the whole environment on our planet would change.

Colorful leaves

When we look at trees in the summer, we see green leaves. What we cannot see is that green leaves are also shades of red, yellow, and orange. We cannot see these other colors because they are covered, or **masked**, by the strong green color in most leaves.

In autumn, the chlorophyll that makes leaves green is destroyed by cold weather. Once the green is gone, the other colors in leaves show through. The red, yellow, and orange leaves that have been covered up by green all summer put on a colorful show before they fall to the ground.

Tree-leaf quiz

Each tree has a unique leaf. With a little practice, you can recognize many kinds of trees by using their leaves as clues. Look carefully at the different leaves pictured on these two pages. Match the listed names to the correct leaves and check page 13 for answers.

The leaves shown are from the following trees: eastern white pine, balsam fir, ginkgo, European white birch, sugar maple, juniper, coconut palm, weeping willow, tamarack, jack pine, white oak, northern white cedar, staghorn sumac, and white spruce.

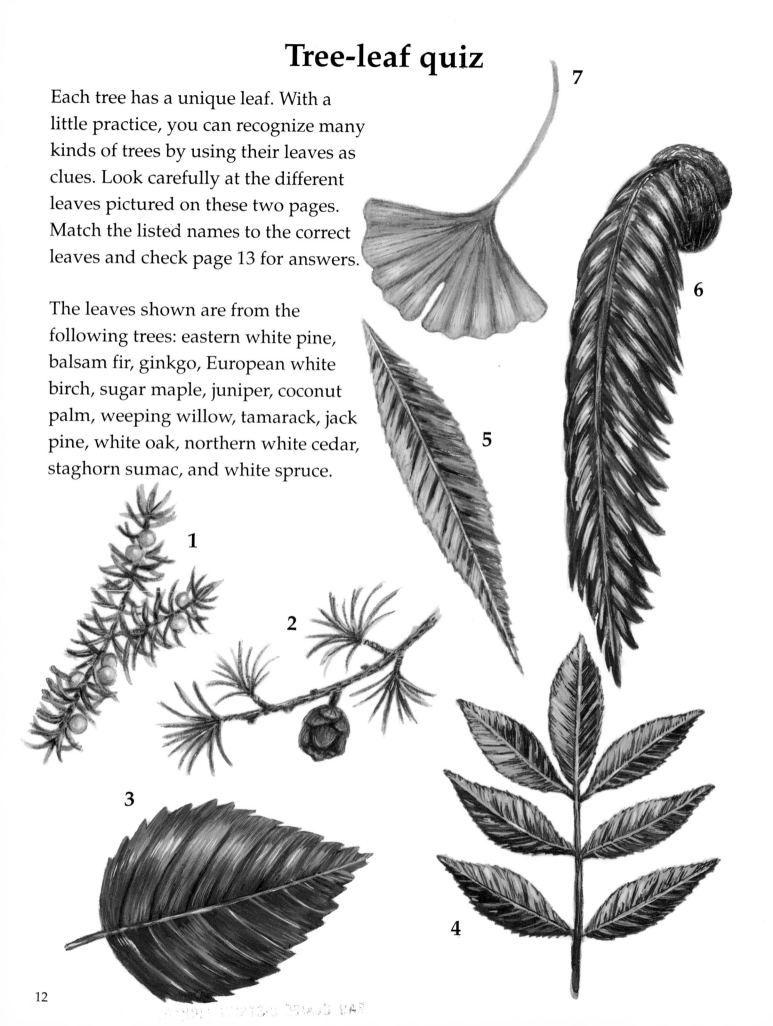

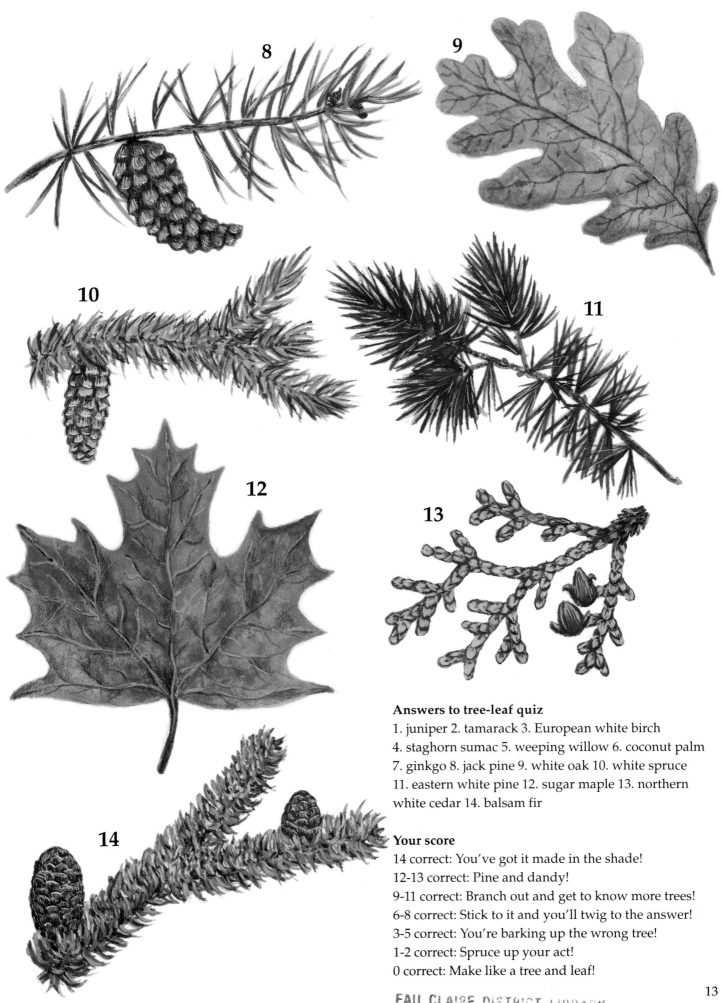

Answers to tree-leaf quiz
1. juniper 2. tamarack 3. European white birch
4. staghorn sumac 5. weeping willow 6. coconut palm
7. ginkgo 8. jack pine 9. white oak 10. white spruce
11. eastern white pine 12. sugar maple 13. northern
white cedar 14. balsam fir

Your score
14 correct: You've got it made in the shade!
12-13 correct: Pine and dandy!
9-11 correct: Branch out and get to know more trees!
6-8 correct: Stick to it and you'll twig to the answer!
3-5 correct: You're barking up the wrong tree!
1-2 correct: Spruce up your act!
0 correct: Make like a tree and leaf!

The story of the ginkgo tree

The ginkgo tree is also known as the maidenhair tree. It keeps its leaves late into autumn. Then the leaves fall all at once.

Katie is wearing gold-plated ginkgo-leaf earrings. They remind her of the beauty of trees. Katie loves trees and writes songs about them. How do you feel about trees?

The **ginkgo** is an ancient tree. It has been on earth since the time of the dinosaurs! For many years, almost everyone believed that there were no more ginkgo trees on earth.

Fortunately, however, a few trees were still alive at a faraway temple in China. For centuries, the monks who lived there carefully looked after the last-remaining gingko trees. The seeds from those trees were used to bring the ginkgo back to parks and gardens all over the world. Today, ginkgos line many city streets.

A symbol of good luck

The ginkgo is a reminder that we must take care of the trees around us. To some, the ginkgo's story of survival is so special that they wear silver- or gold-plated ginkgo leaves on necklaces or earrings. The ginkgo leaf has become a symbol of good luck!

Tree poetry

Each year that the ginkgo survives gives people hope for the future of all trees. To remind yourselves just how much you care for trees, you and your friends can decorate your room or classroom with poetry-filled ginkgo leaves you have made yourselves.

Write poems about trees on pieces of construction paper that have been cut out in the fanlike shape of ginkgo leaves.

I love this tree!

The following poems were written by children. They all begin with the line "I love this tree!" How do you express your love for trees? Do you recycle paper? Have you hugged a tree?

People and trees in harmony

I love this tree;
This tree loves me.
It protects me from the hot, hot sun;
It lets me hide when I'm having fun.
The big 3Rs help save my tree:
I won't use paper plates or cups
I'll keep my blue box filled to the top
So the birds can live in the trees.
Then nature and people can live
In harmony.
Derek Organ, age 8

Dance with us and the wind

I love this tree—
Its leaves are dark and lovely,
Moving, rustling, shaking,
Talking to me and the other trees,
They're singing.
Join us
Swing with us
Dance with us and the wind.
Manvinder Sahota, age 9

A place that's all my own

I love this tree!
It's my favorite climbing spot.
There is a branch I call my throne,
It's a place that's all my own.
I can sit here all day long
And no one ever knows I'm here—
It's just me and my tree and the wind.
Adelaide Wong, age 8

A little tree popped up

I love this tree
Because it is a peach tree.
Peaches were my favorite fruit
From the beginning.
I had a little pit
I planted it in the ground
I waited and waited
Then a little tree popped up!
Now I'll have peaches forever.
I love this tree!
Stephanie Stojanowski, age 9

Flowers, fruits, and cones

The making of new trees is called **reproduction**. Reproduction in most trees begins with flowers. Tree flowers have male and female parts. A dusty substance called **pollen** is carried from the male parts of one flower to the female parts of another flower. When this happens, a seed is made. Tree seeds can grow inside nuts, fruits, or berries. Each tree seed is able to grow into a tree.

Carried by the wind

Trees with cones do not have flowers; they have flower-like parts instead. These trees depend on the wind to carry their pollen so that male and female parts can join. The seeds then grow inside the female cones.

Birds, animals, and the wind carry pollen from flower to flower. They also scatter the seeds that later become trees.

mature female cone

young cones

seeds

Scattering seeds

Trees are rooted in the ground and cannot move around to plant their seeds in good spots. This means that they have to depend on the wind, animals, and insects to do the job for them! Trees produce colorful, delicious fruit, nuts, or berries that make tasty meals for many creatures. A crow, for example, might swallow a cherry and then fly away. Later, it will get rid of the cherry pit in its droppings. In the spring, that same crow might fly over the tiny cherry tree that it planted!

Many kinds of flowers

People all over the world look forward to seeing and smelling the beautiful blossoms of trees. Most trees have flowers, but not all are scented and colorful. Some flowers are so tiny that they can only be seen with a magnifying glass. Other tree flowers have two separate parts that hardly look like true flowers at all! On the hazel tree there are long tassel flowers called **catkins**.

a catkin

Most broadleaved trees have flowers or fruit or both. The tree below has tiny berries.

A tree is born

Baby trees, called **seedlings**, sprout from the tiny seeds dropped by their parents. Coniferous seedlings sprout from the seeds found in cones. Peaches and plums have one seed inside each piece of fruit, whereas apples and lemons have many seeds.

Only a few seeds will live and grow to become a year old. Even fewer seeds develop into mature trees. Most of the seeds land in places where they cannot survive. Many are eaten or trampled by animals. Each tree that survives is a miracle of nature.

1. Each seed contains the food it needs to get it started in life. The seed uses this first meal to sprout a root and start growing a small stem.

*2. It takes about two weeks for a seed from a deciduous tree to make two stubby little leaves. These leaves are called **seed leaves**. They push aside the case in which they have been curled up and reach for the sun.*

3. During the next week, the seedling sprouts its first true leaves. These leaves look like the leaves on the parent tree. For the following two months, the roots and stem grow and get stronger.

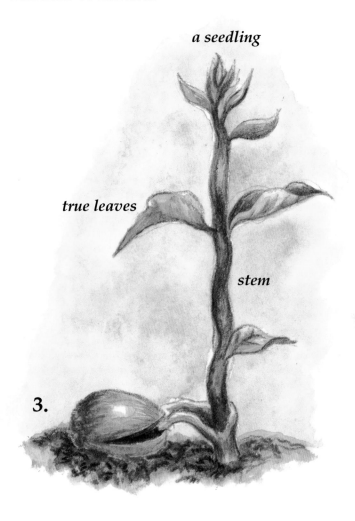

a seedling

true leaves

stem

3.

1.

seed leaves

2.

If the seedling survives its first winter, it will start its second year as a new baby tree. It will grow buds on its tiny branches, and its stem will be covered with a thin, delicate bark.

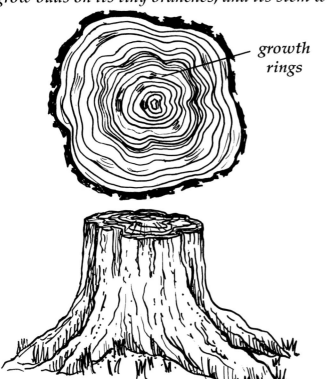

growth rings

A growing tree

When you look at a tree that has been cut down, you will see many growth rings inside the trunk. Each growth ring stands for one of the tree's birthdays. If you count them all, you will know how old a tree is. When you see a thick ring, it means that the tree had an excellent growth year. A narrow ring means that the tree had a year of slow growth. As a tree's trunk, branches, and roots get fatter, the tips of its twigs and roots grow longer.

How a tree dies

Most healthy trees live for many years. Some survive for centuries! But, in the life of every tree, there comes a time when the tree weakens. Insects make small wounds in its trunk and branches. Plants grow on its bark and drain the strength of the tree.

After a number of years, the tree cannot fight diseases and attacking creatures anymore. The sap no longer flows in its trunk and branches, and the leaves do not burst into bud in the spring. When these things stop happening, the tree has died.

When its bark is damaged, a tree can dry out. Small creatures attack the injured bark and can cause the tree to become sick and die.

Moss and fungi start growing on the surfaces of rotting trees.

20

Animals and insects live under rotting trees and find food there. This fallen dead tree is so enormous that its trunk is bigger than the children who are examining it.

Back to the soil

The leaves, twigs, and flaking bark that fall to the ground break down and turn into a black, crumbly substance called **humus**. Humus is rich in the foods that plants need for growing.

Food and shelter

Toads **hibernate** under the fallen logs of dead trees. Worms, snails, wood ants, beetles, and many other kinds of insects live and feed in decaying logs and leaves. Ferns, mosses, fungi, and plants grow in the rotting trunk.

Look at a dead log with a magnifying glass. Can you see any insects or plants living on it?

Dangers to trees

Acid rain

There are more people living on our earth than ever before. All these people contribute to the pollution of the land, air, and water. Pollution is dangerous to trees as well as people.

An especially harmful substance to trees is called **acid rain**. Acid rain is formed when gases from factories and cars mix with water droplets that are floating in the air. These tiny droplets form rain or snow that is like vinegar! Acid rain hurts the leaves of trees and damages the soil around tree roots. Eventually, it can kill trees.

Killing the forests

In many areas of the world, people are cutting down forests without planting new trees. Killing forests is very harmful to the environment. The plants and animals that used to live in the forest often disappear forever.

Cutting down large areas of forest can even change the weather! Sometimes the rain stops and never returns, and the area turns into a desert. The soil that used to be held in place by thousands of tree roots is washed away. It ends up in rivers, making them so muddy that fish and plants die.

Forest fires kill thousands of trees each year, and the smoke damages large areas around the burning forests. The smoke in this picture is from a forest fire that is hundreds of kilometers in the distance. Many forest fires are caused by careless campers.

Clearcutting

There are many ways of cutting down forests. One of the most destructive to the environment is called **clearcutting**. Logging companies that clearcut forests chop down every tree and then collect only the trees that they can sell. Large areas that have been clearcut often turn into deserts.

Insect and animal damage

Hundreds of kinds of insects and animals can live on a single healthy tree. They munch on the leaves, twigs and bark, and suck sap. Most trees survive this attack, but some trees die.

Forest fires

Some forest fires are caused by lightning, but most are started by careless people. Forest fires can pollute the air by sending huge clouds of smoke into the sky. It may take years for plants, animals, and trees to return to burnt areas.

Sick trees

When a tree has deep-green leaves, it is a sign that it is healthy. A sick tree usually has yellowish or brown leaves. Sometimes insects spread diseases from one tree to another, but many tree diseases are carried by the wind.

How you can help trees

You know that there are many ways in which trees help you, but do you realize that trees need your help in return? Anyone can take steps to help preserve the world's trees. Here are some simple things you can do:

• **Reuse paper whenever you can and then recycle it.** When you need to buy paper products, buy ones that use recycled materials. When paper is wasted, more trees must be cut down to make new paper.

This living Christmas tree is decorated with live kids! Do you buy a cut tree at Christmas time? Has your family thought about decorating a living tree?

You can save trees by recycling cardboard and newspapers. Most schools also have fine-paper recycling bins to collect the paper that you use in school.

• **Do not waste trees!** At Christmas time, most people used to buy cut trees that ended up being thrown out. Today, many people do not want to waste trees this way. Some families are now buying artificial trees, and others are choosing living trees that can be planted afterwards. In many cities, you can rent living Christmas trees that you return to be planted. Do you decorate a cut tree? Has your family looked into renting a living tree at Christmas time?

• **Be a forest tourist.** If you visited a forest, you and your family would probably spend money in the area. When people make money from tourism, they are not as eager to cut down forests for lumber.

• **Do not buy items with a lot of paper packaging.** Tell the manager at the store that you will not buy the item until it is sold with less waste around it.

• **Avoid buying items made with rare or precious woods such as teak.** Tropical rainforests must be killed to harvest these types of trees.

• **Plant a tree.** People all over the world are planting trees to help replace the ones that are being cut down. You can plant a tree at home or at school. You will feel proud when you see your tree grow. Your tree will provide a home for animals, birds, and insects. It will help clean the air. Planting a tree is a wonderful way to help the environment. Make plans to plant one this spring.

• **Teach others to love trees, too.** The more information people have about trees, the more they will want to preserve the world's forests. Ask your teacher or principal to hold a tree-appreciation week at school. Write poems and songs about trees and draw pictures of them. Put on plays about trees. Tell some tree jokes. Make posters that tell people how they can save trees.

Pretend you are a tree and branch out!

The troll and the tree

All the trees on Troll Mountain are enchanted. Once, as I wandered through the ancient forest near the peak, I stopped to look up at a grandfather tree and asked, "What magical secrets do you hide, Old One?" Since I received no answer, I sat down with my back to the tree for a short rest and looked around. It was a truly beautiful day!

Not far in front of me, a thick bush grew at the base of a high cliff wall. Suddenly, the bush began to move as though something was behind it. I thought that the bush must be hiding a cave from which some animal was about to emerge. I sat very still.

A moment later, two hands with long, white, almost snakelike fingers appeared and parted the bush like a curtain. My mouth dropped open as a wondrous face appeared. "A troll!" I thought, remembering where I was.

His face wasn't ugly—just a bit different. The troll had no eyes, of course, for creatures who live under-ground have no need of them—but he did have a nose. In fact, it was a huge nose that was bright blue.

The troll, who was the size of a seven-year-old boy, stepped from the bush and turned his head slowly left and then right. He was carefully listening with his very large, willow-leaf ears, whose color reminded me of oranges.

The troll sniffed the air deeply. "Ahhhh!" he said and waddled across the forest floor on his short stubby legs. He seemed to be enjoying himself immensely, giggling every time he bumped into something. He was a

young troll, perhaps on his first trip to the earth's surface.

Finally, the troll bumped into the tree under which I sat, and stopped as if he had found what he was looking for. He gave the ancient tree a fierce hug and hummed with delight. Then the little fellow explored every bit of the rough bark with his long, white fingers, from the ground up to as high as his stubby arms could reach.

Next, he put an orange ear against the tree's trunk and listened for a long time, smiling and humming every once in a while. The troll—whom, I decided, I liked very much—touched the rough bark gently with his long, bright-pink tongue and giggled at the taste. Finally, my little troll gave a good-bye hug to the old tree and waddled back to the high rock wall. He stepped through the bush and was gone.

As I made my spellbound way out of the forest, I realized that trees only hide their mysteries from those, like me, who do not truly know them. That day, my little troll had shown me his special way of getting to know the forest, and I have practiced it ever since. Now, every tree I meet seems as enchanted as the trees on Troll Mountain.

How to "troll" a tree

You can get to know a tree the troll way, too! It is a lot of fun, and who knows what secrets you will learn?

A mystery trek

To get started, all you need is a friend, a blindfold, and a stethoscope, if you can borrow one. Go to a forested area with your friend and choose a spot with lots of trees but not too much underbrush. Have your friend tie the blindfold on you and then turn you around and around. Your friend will now take you by the arm. It is his or her job to make sure you do not fall down. He will lead you to a tree on a roundabout route. On the way there, he will warn you to duck under branches or step over logs and stones. These may be imaginary branches and stones made up by your partner, for the aim is to make sure that you are totally lost! Before long, you will arrive at the chosen tree.

Learning to use your senses

Don't try to keep track of where you are, as that will only interfere with the workings of your senses. The troll-way of meeting a tree requires listening to the senses that we rarely use because we rely on our eyes so much.

Your friend will lead you on a mystery trek through the wilderness.

He will give you false clues, such as asking you to duck so you do not bump into a branch.

Feel the tree

Once you have come to your tree, place your hands on it. Feel the tree, as the troll did, from the ground up to as high as you can reach. Is the bark smooth or rough? Hard or soft? Damp or dry? Cool or warm?

Listen to the sounds of life

Use your other senses, too. With practice, you can tell the difference between a deciduous and coniferous tree by the sound of the wind in the branches overhead. If you have a stethoscope (our ears aren't as good as a troll's) and listen to the tree's trunk, you may hear sounds made by a living tree. You may also hear the insects that inhabit it. Smell the tree. You may be able to recognize the tree by its own special perfume.

Find the tree on your own

Now it's time for your partner to take you back to your starting point in a roundabout way. Once there, take off your blindfold and find the tree on your own. Your friend can guide you by telling you if you are "getting warm," or "getting cold," but give yourself a chance to find your tree without too many clues. You may surprise yourself! Once you have found your tree and given it a hug, it will be your friend's turn to troll a tree.

Feel the tree and remember its bark pattern.

Smell the tree and listen to the sounds inside it.

Make friends with a tree

Sketch your tree in winter and summer.

These children found a nest in their tree.

After you have trolled a tree, you may want to visit it from time to time, just as you would visit a friend. If the tree is not near your home, choose another tree that you find particularly interesting and become friends with it. Here are some ways you can get to know your tree:

Sketch it. Take a pad of recycled paper and a pencil with you and make a sketch of the tree. What is its shape? What kind of fruit, nuts, or seeds does it grow? Draw the outline of one leaf or make a sketch of the needles on one tiny branch.

Examine it. Have any animals made their homes in the tree? Look in the branches for squirrels or bird nests. Examine the trunk for holes made by insects or birds. Study the leaves and bark for insect homes. Are there any creatures living in or around the tree's roots?

Take note of any damage to the tree caused by storms, insects, animals, or people. Does the tree seem sturdy and full of life? Are its leaves green and undamaged? Are the branches and trunk healthy? Does the tree have many scars?

Measure it. Take a measuring tape and measure around the trunk of your tree. Estimate the height of the tree by standing with your back to it. With a piece of chalk, make a little mark on the bark above your head. How many times would your marked height fit into the tree's height? If you guessed three, then mark down that the tree is about three times as big as you are and calculate the height by multiplying your height times three.

Measure yourself against the tree.

Make a bark rubbing of your tree. Hold a piece of recycled paper up against the trunk of your tree. Using a thick crayon, gently rub the surface. The wax from the crayon will make marks on the paper when it rubs across the bark underneath. When you are finished, you will have a picture that shows the exact pattern of the bark on your tree. It is like the tree's fingerprint. Make bark rubbings of several types of trees and compare their patterns to that of your tree.

Are any animals living in your tree?

Hug your new friend. Take a few moments to think about why your tree is important to you. Give it a big hug. Once you have made friends with a tree, you will have joined thousands of other people who have started taking special interest in trees. Aren't trees simply wonderful?

Make a bark rubbing of your tree friend.

Glossary

acid rain Rain that has become polluted by gases from factories and cars

carbon dioxide A gas present in the atmosphere. Humans breathe it out, and trees breathe it in.

chlorophyll The green-coloring matter in leaves and plants

clearcutting The process of chopping down every tree in an area, collecting only certain trees, and leaving the rest to rot

coniferous Cone bearing

deciduous Describing a type of tree that sheds its leaves annually

environment The surroundings that affect the existence of living beings

evergreen A type of tree that has green leaves throughout the year

hibernation A state of inactivity, usually during the winter

humus Dark-colored decayed vegetable matter that forms the nutritious part of soil

nutrition The process of nourishing or being nourished

oxygen A colorless, odorless gas in the air that is necessary for the survival of living things. Trees breathe out large quantities of oxygen.

pollen The yellow powdery dust of flowering plants—the male part of the fertilization process

pollution The state of being impure or dirty

rainforest A dense forest found in a tropical region that gets a lot of rain

reproduction The production of offspring

root hair A tiny threadlike root that sprouts in a tree's roots. It absorbs water and food from the soil and passes them on to the tree's main roots.

sap The fluid food that circulates in a tree and makes it grow. Sunlight and chlorophyll combine to change air and water into sap.

seedling A young plant grown from a seed

1 2 3 4 5 6 7 8 9 0 Printed in USA 1 0 9 8 7 6 5 4 3 2

Index

acid rain 22
banyan tree 6
bark 4, 7, 9, 19, 20, 21, 23, 27, 29, 30, 31
bark rubbing 31
branches 6, 19, 20, 28, 30
broadleaved trees 9, 17
carbon dioxide 11
chlorophyll 11
Christmas trees 24
clearcutting 23
cones 8, 14, 16, 29
coniferous trees 8, 18, 29
dead trees 20-21
deciduous trees 8, 9, 18, 29
diseases 20, 23
environment 4, 11, 22, 25
evergreens 8, 18
flowers 4, 6, 16, 17
forest fires 23
forests 6, 11, 22, 25, 27, 28
fruit 4, 6, 7, 16, 30
ginkgo tree 12, 14-15
leaves 4, 6, 8, 9, 10, 11, 14, 15, 18, 20, 22, 23, 30
logging 23
oxygen 5, 11, 25
packaging 25
paper 5, 24
planting trees 25
pollen 16
pollution 22, 23
rainforests 4, 6, 25
recycling 24, 30, 31
reproduction 16
roots 4, 6, 9, 18, 19, 22, 30
sap 4, 11, 20, 23
seedlings 18, 19
seeds 4, 7, 16, 18, 30
soil 4, 6, 22
tree poetry 15
tree-leaf quiz 12-13
troll and the tree, The 26-27
trunks 6, 19, 20, 21, 27
water 4, 5, 9